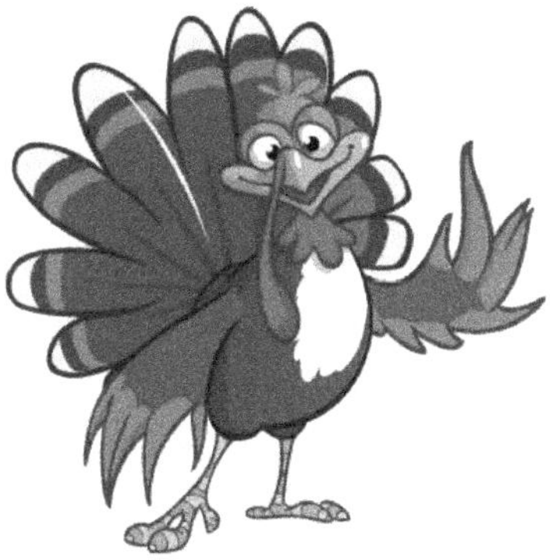

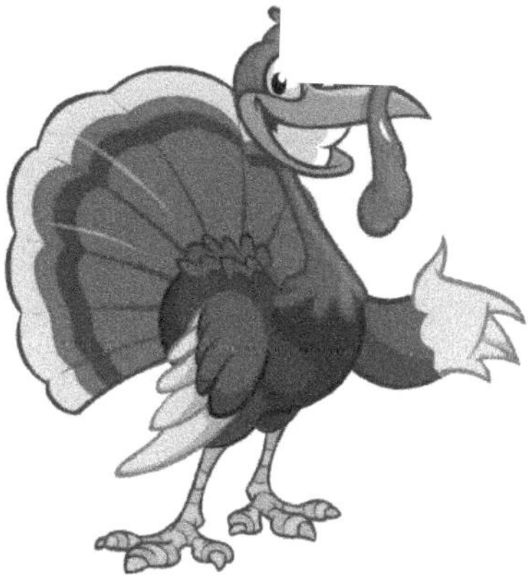

Este libro pertenece a

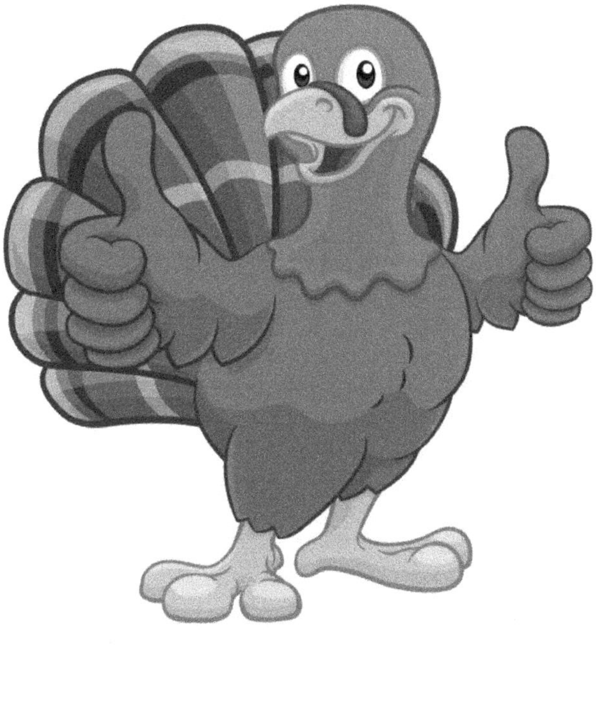

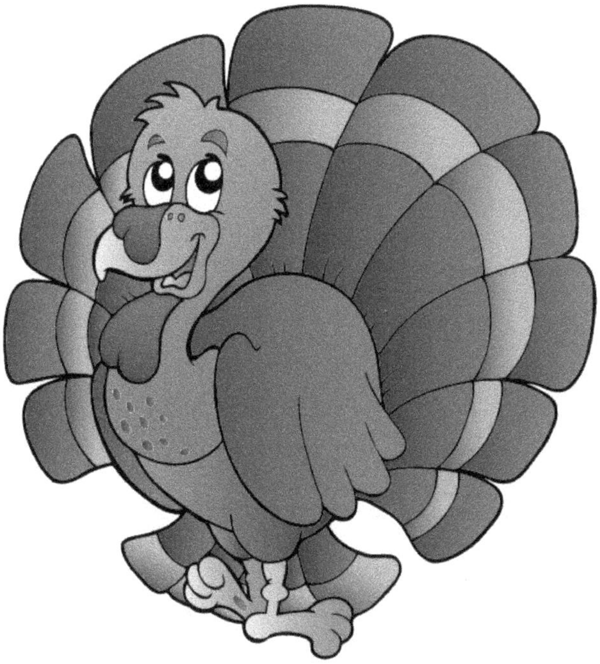

Note

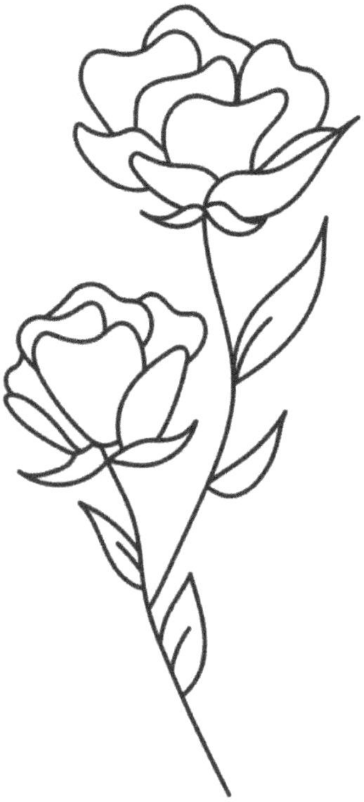

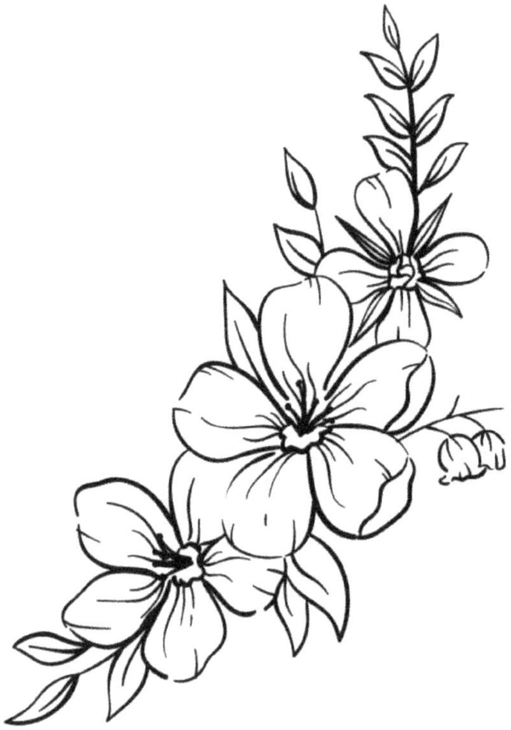

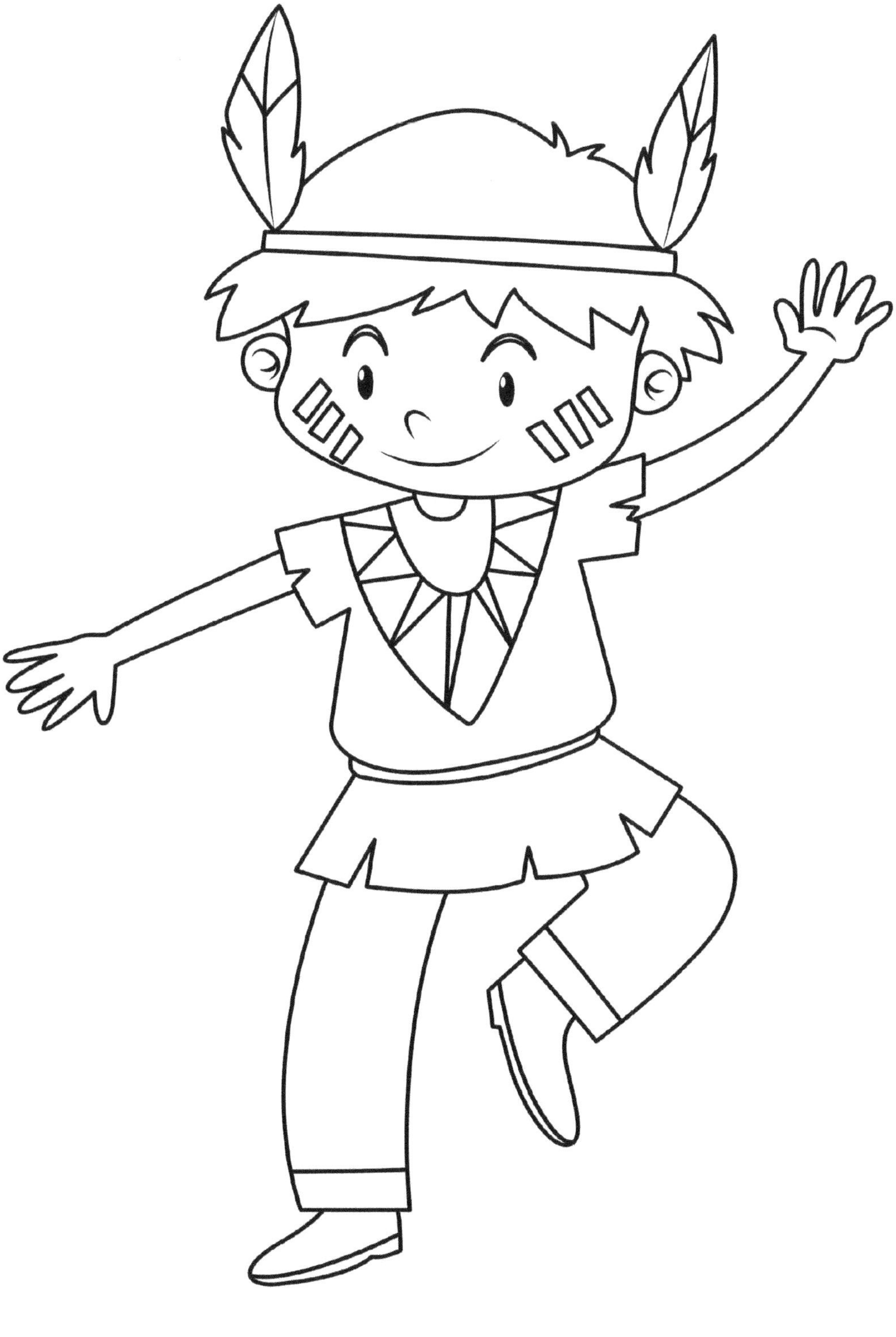

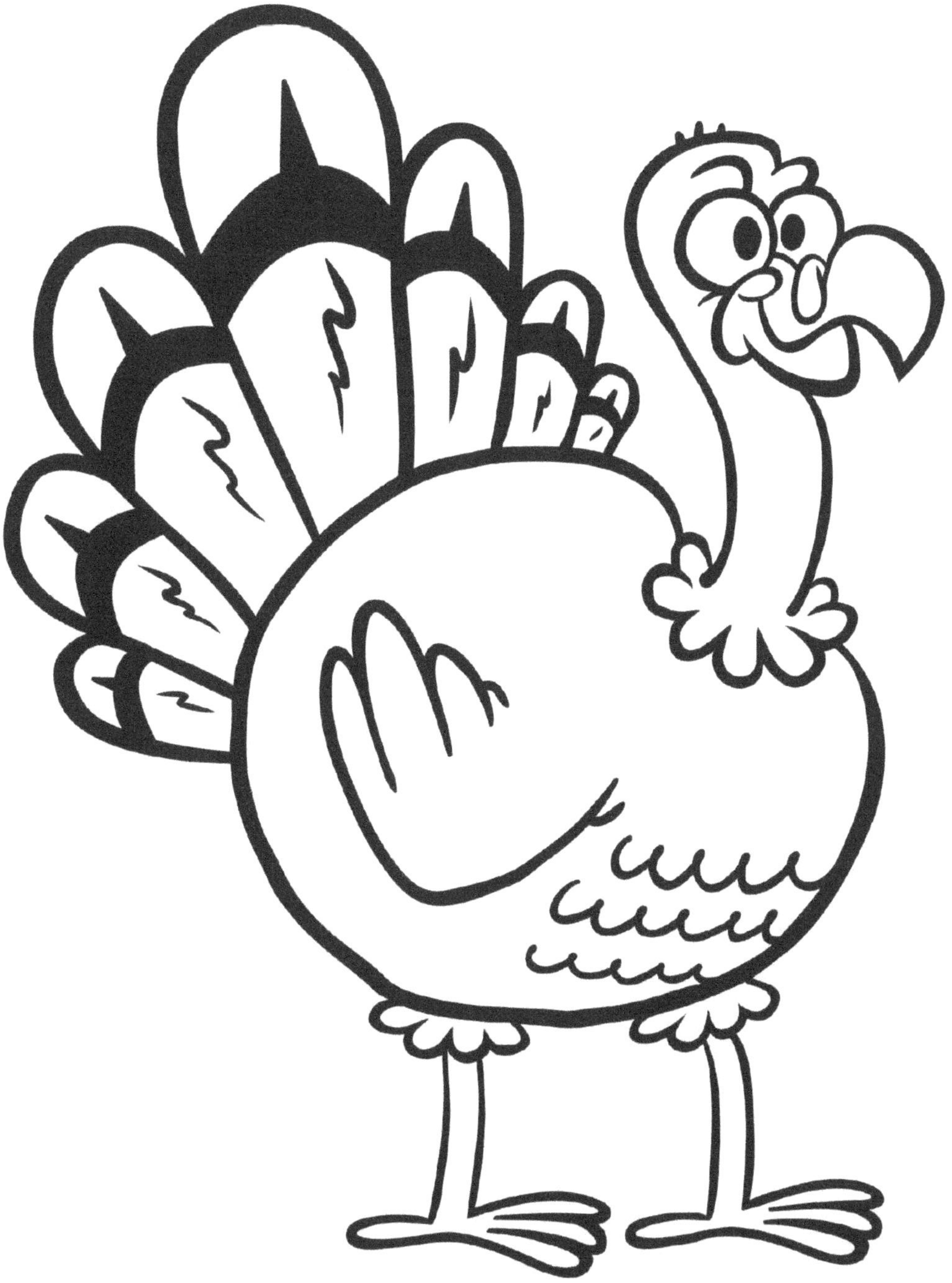

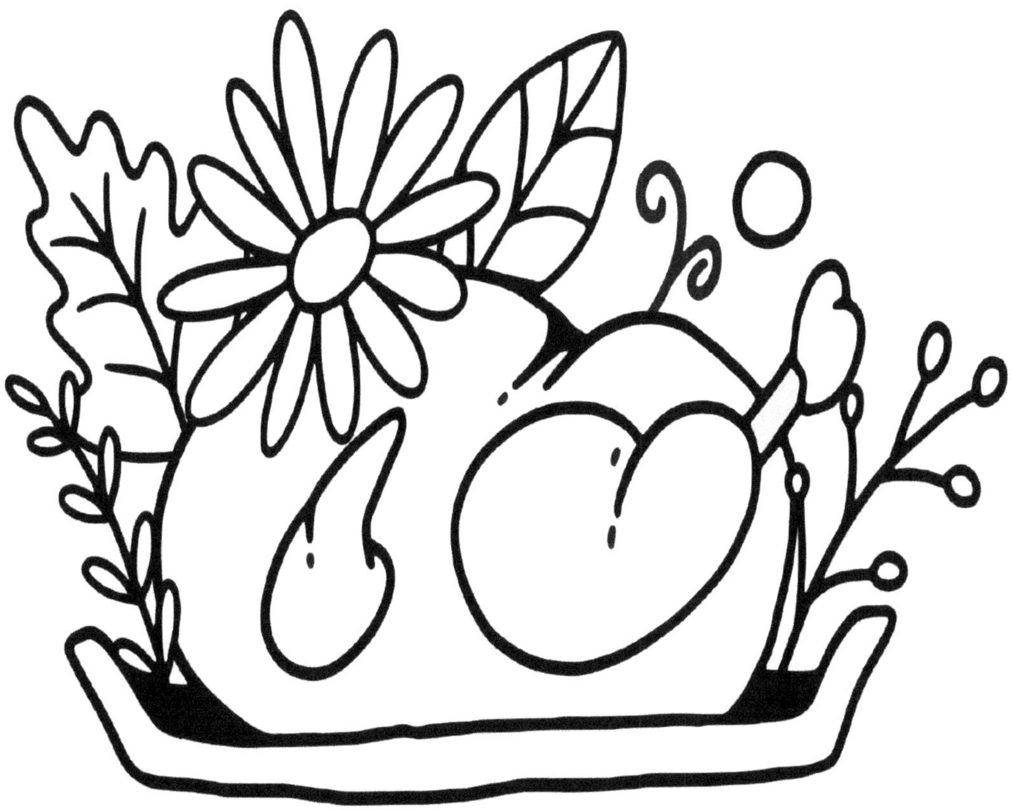

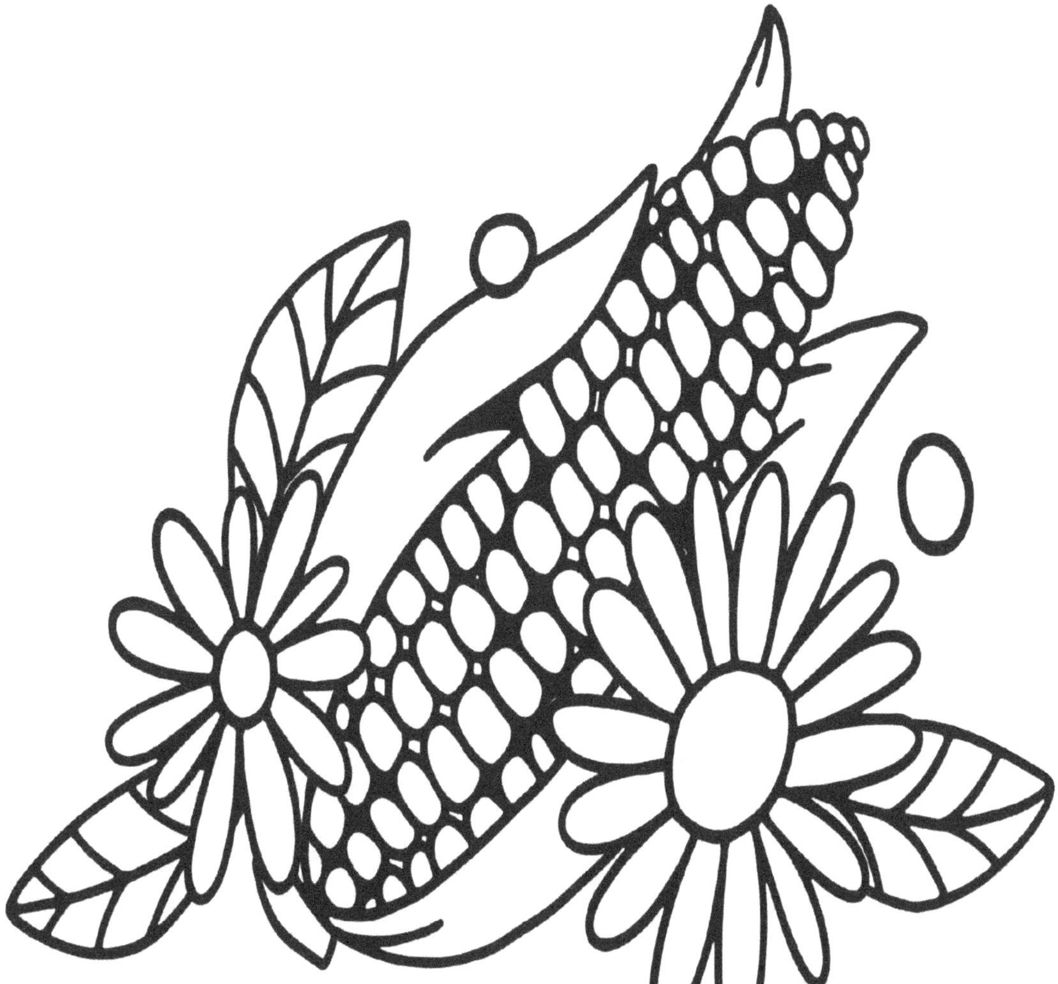

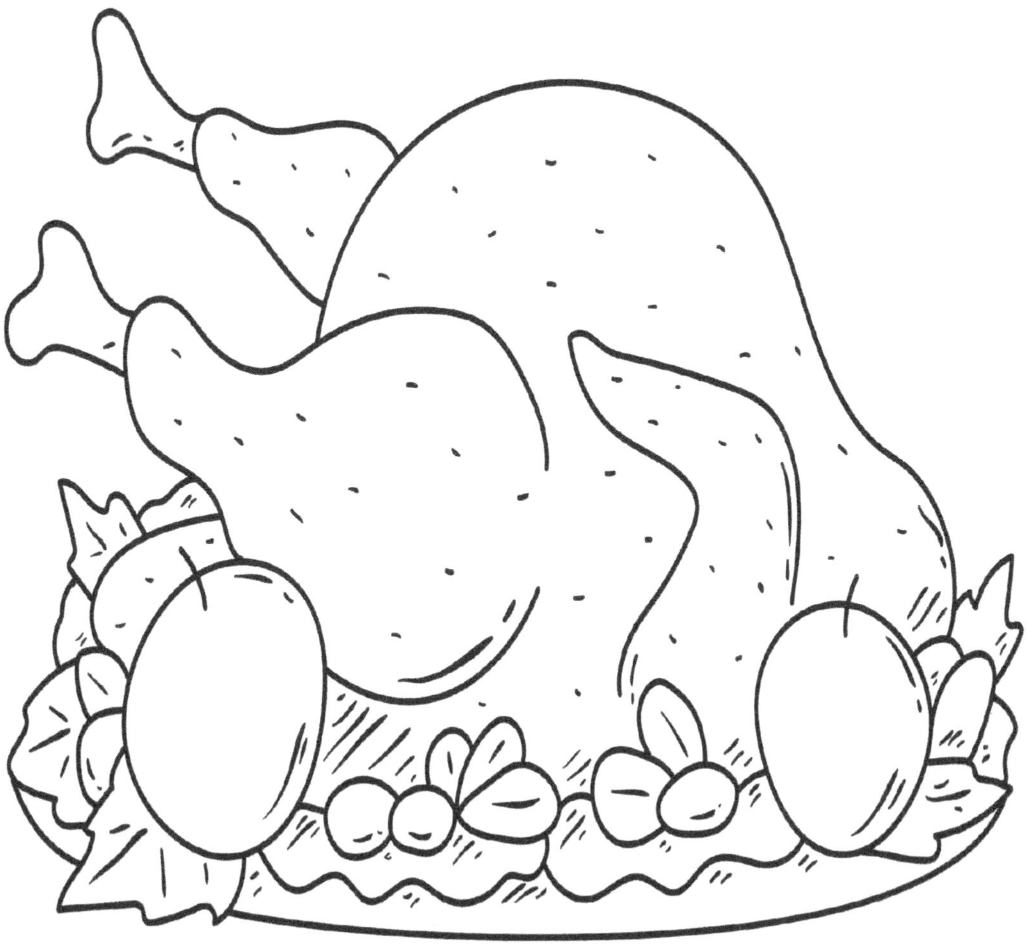

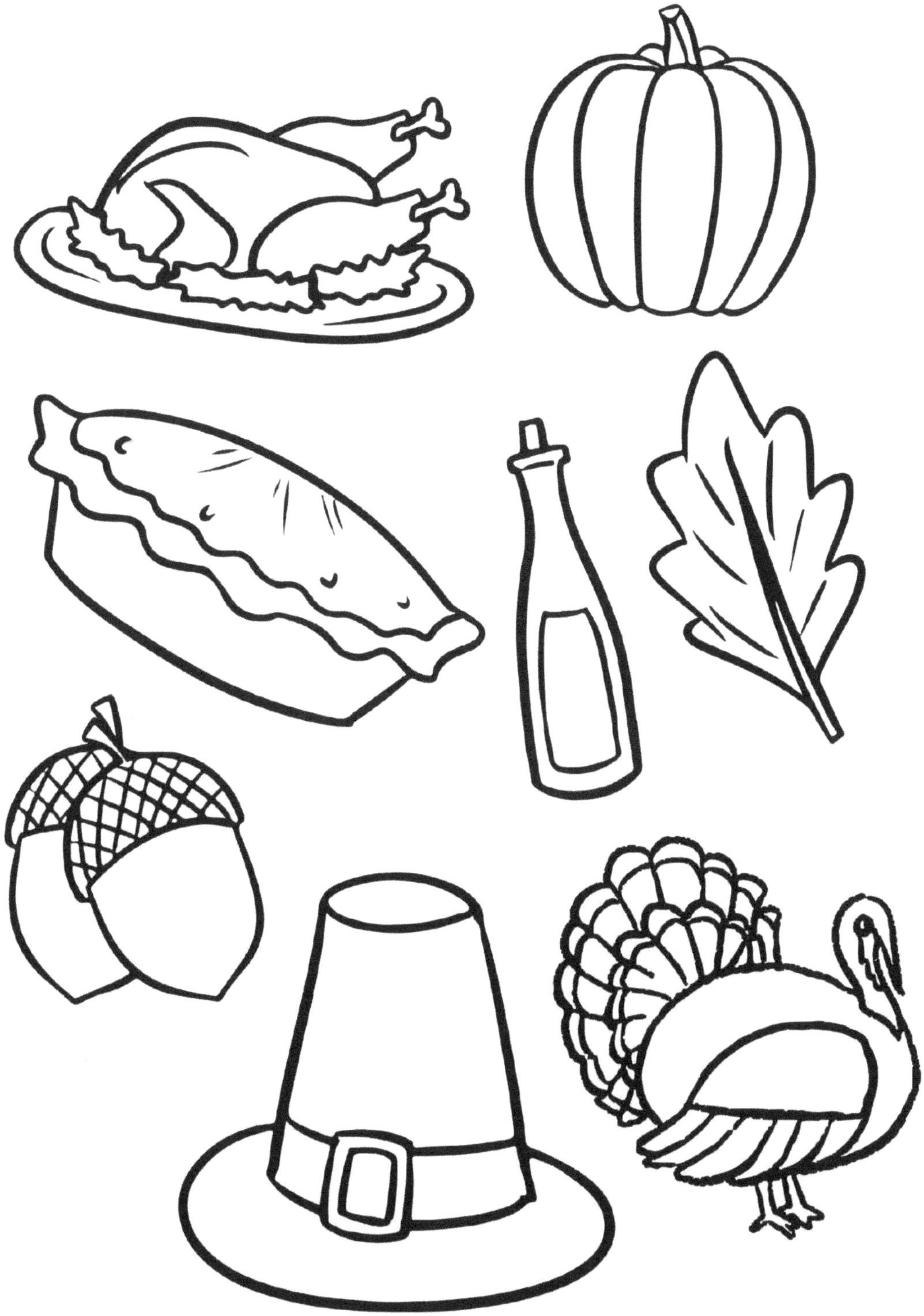

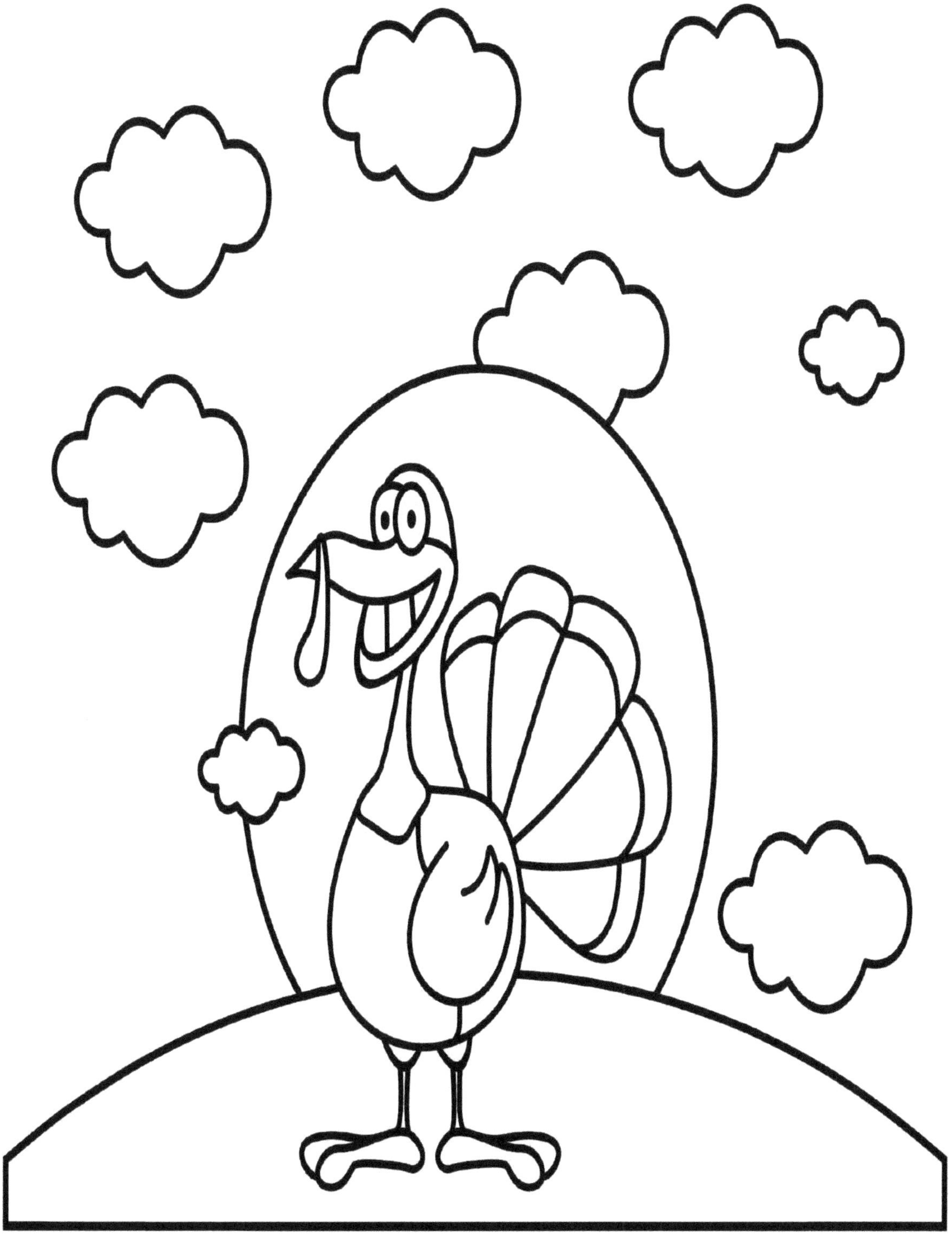

THANKS
GIVING
DOODLE

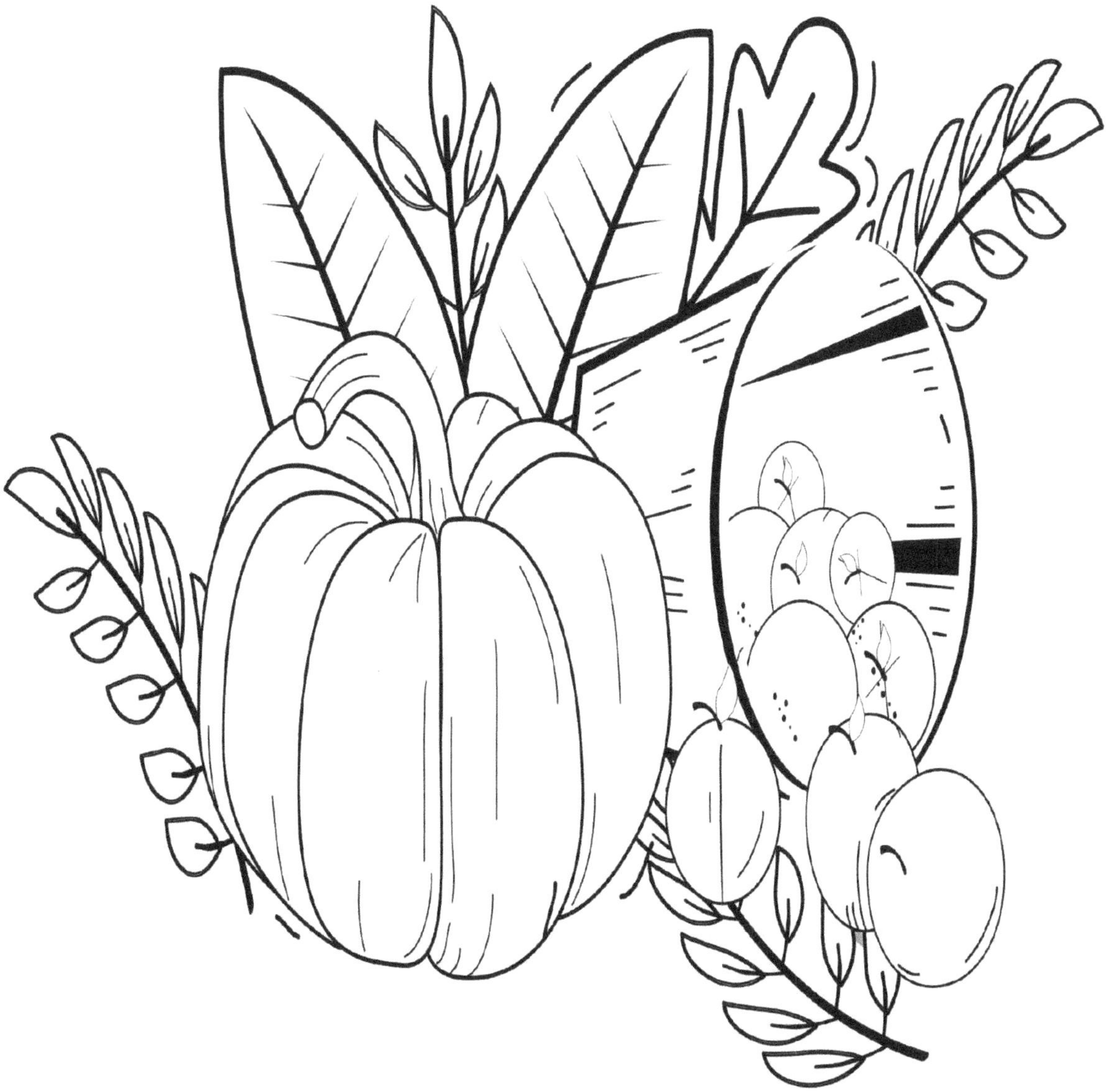

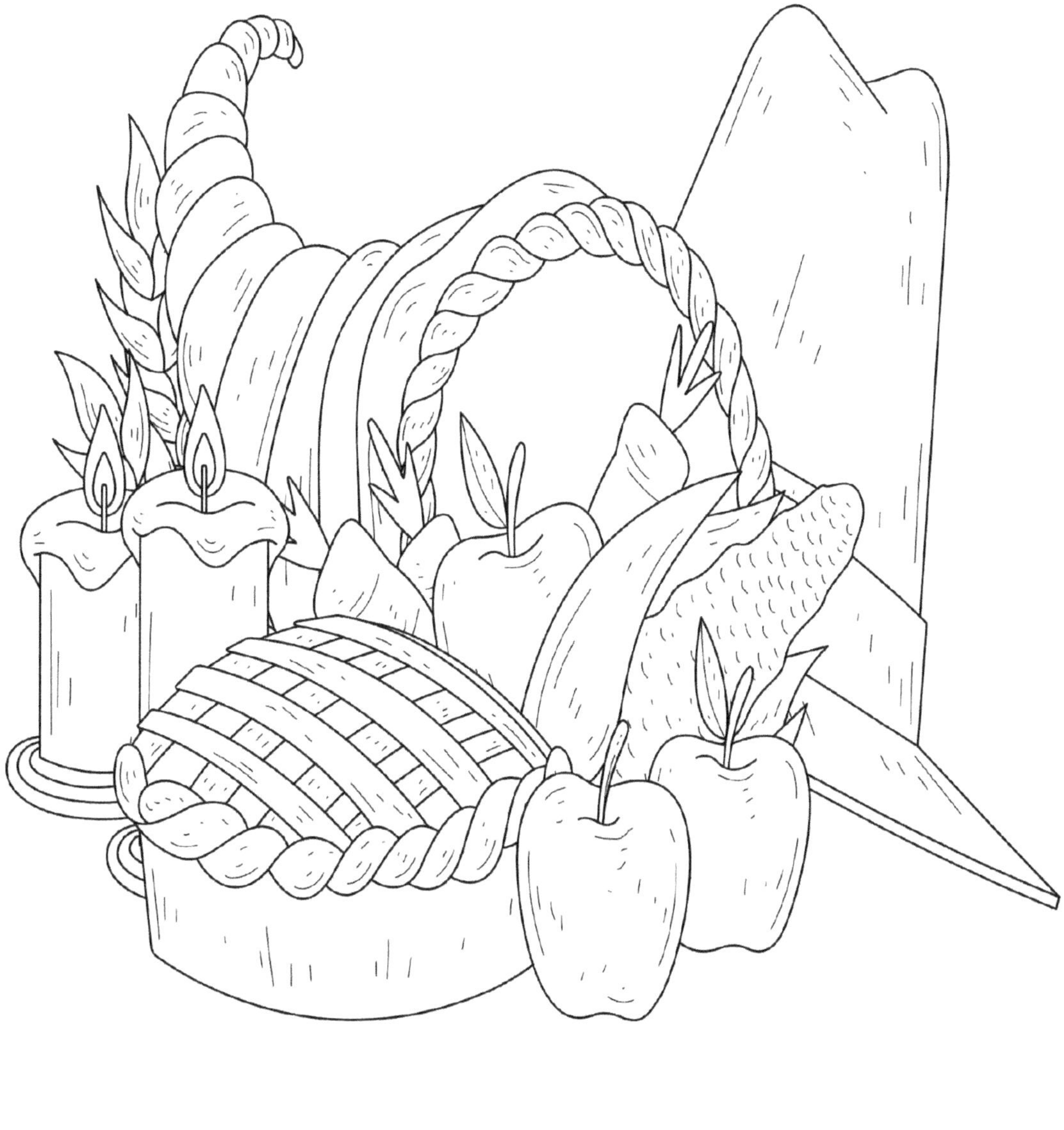

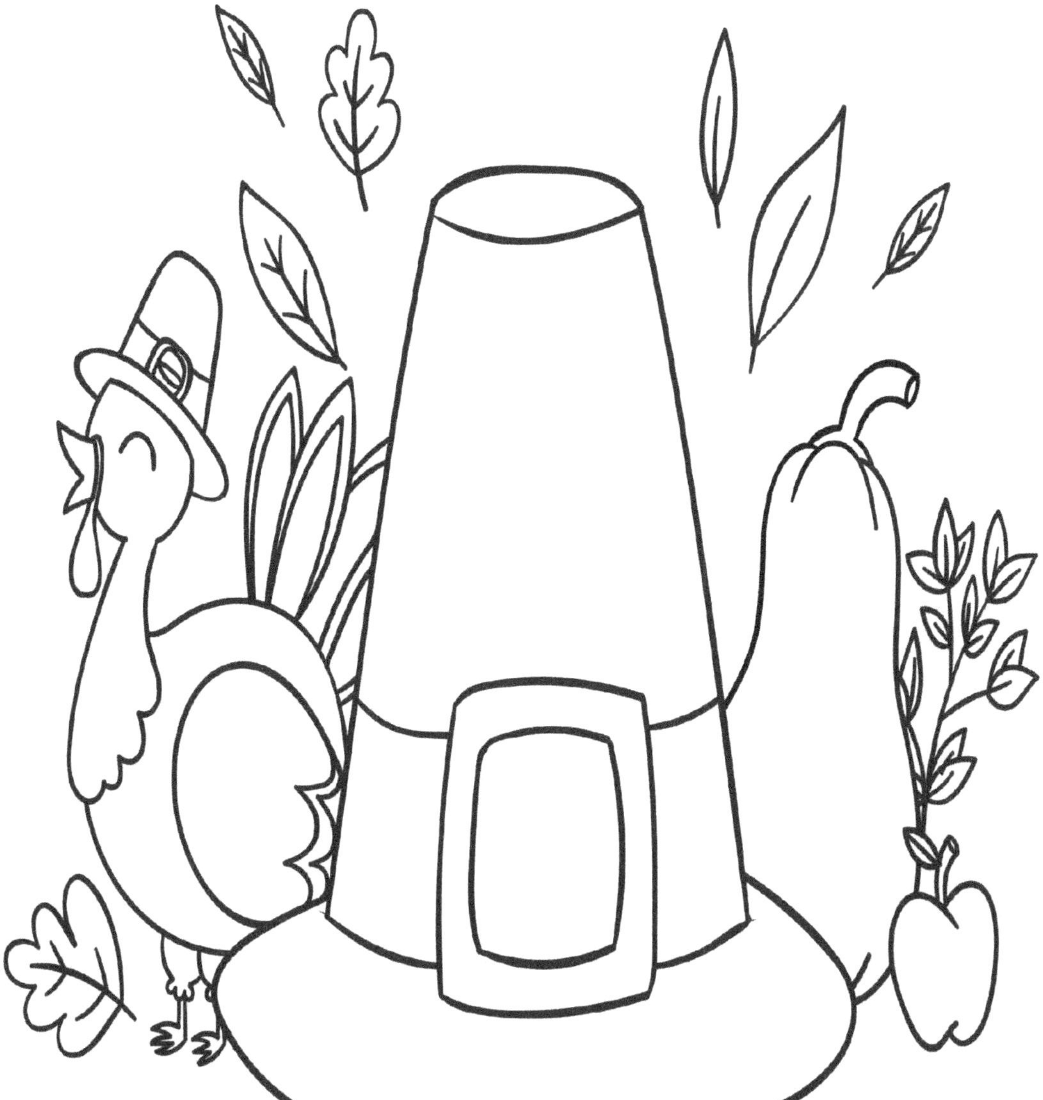

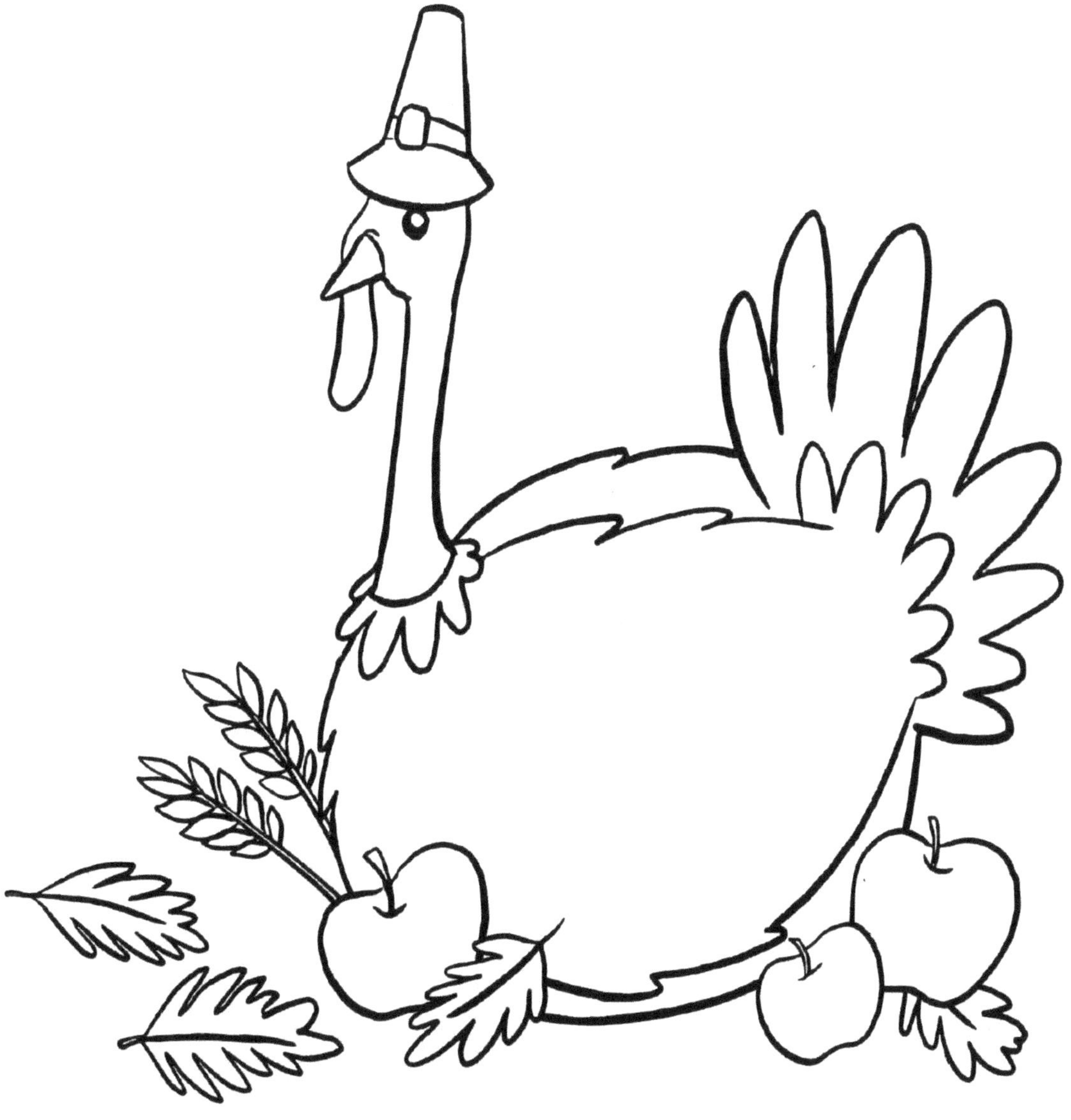

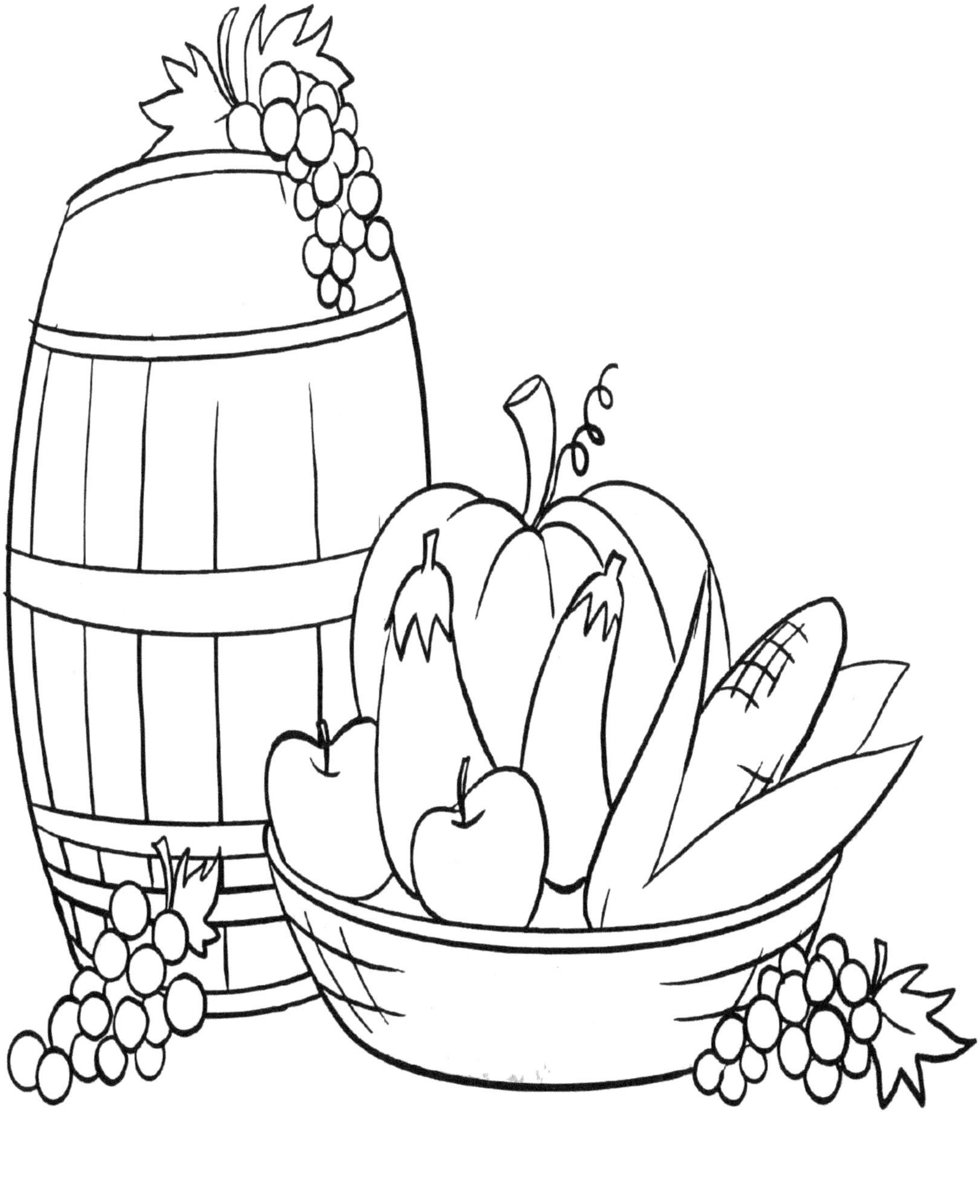

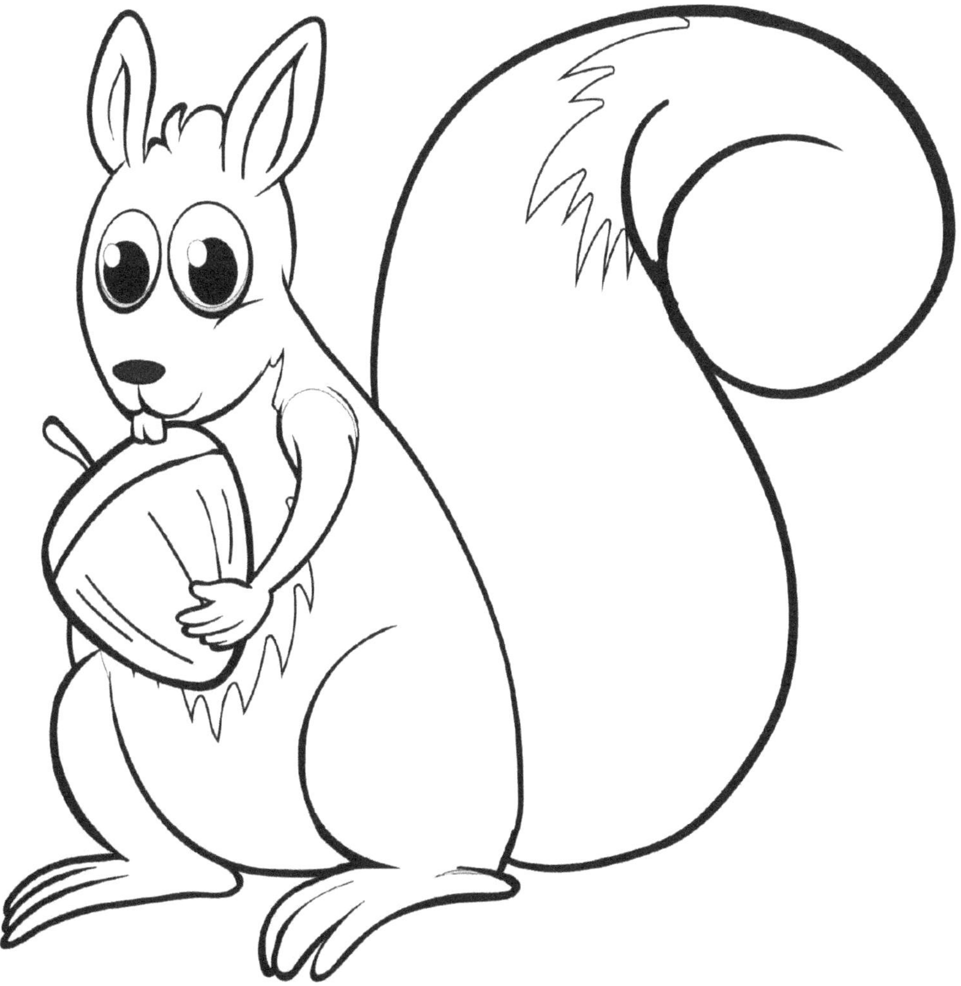

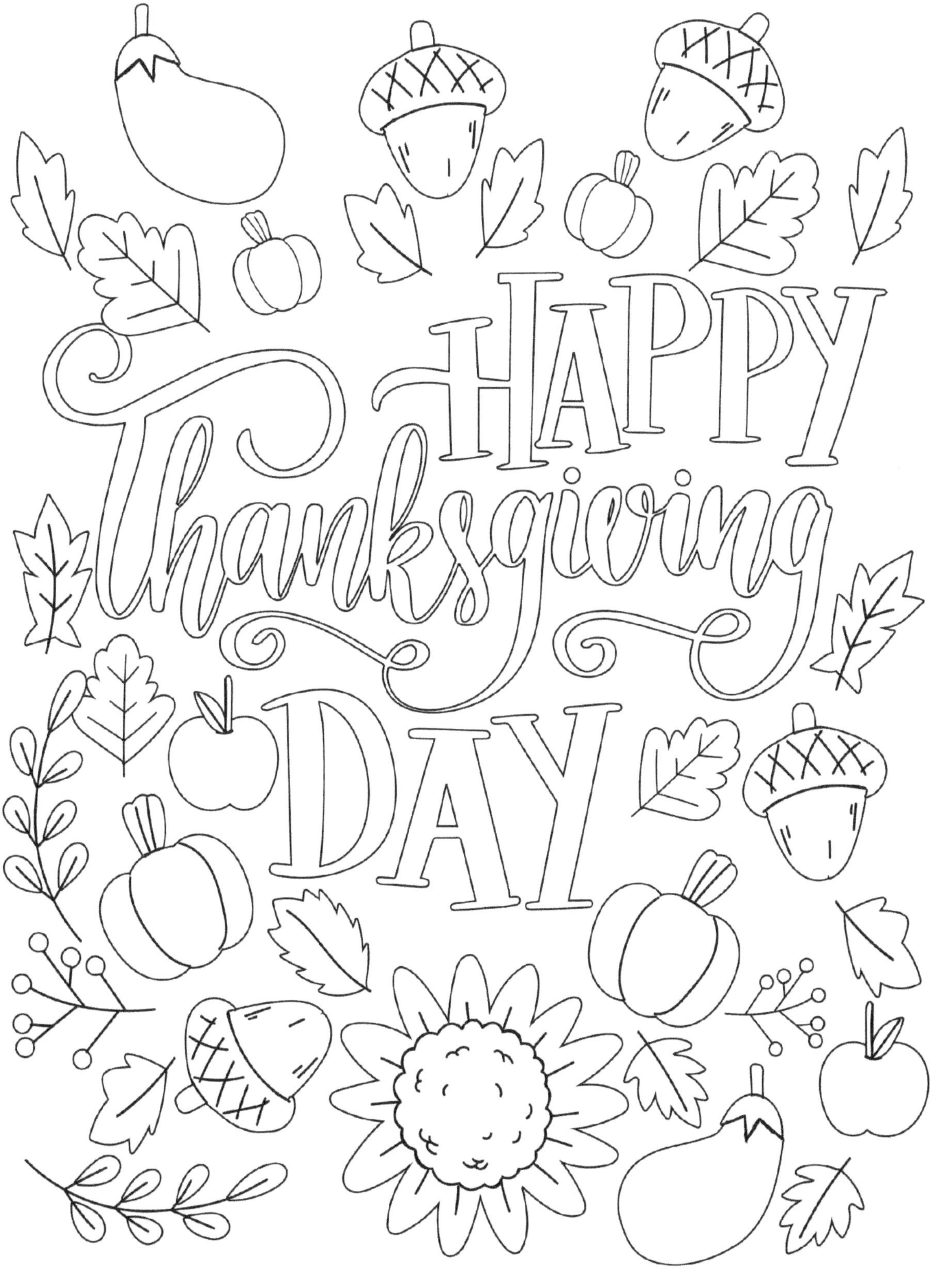
Happy
Thanksgiving
Day

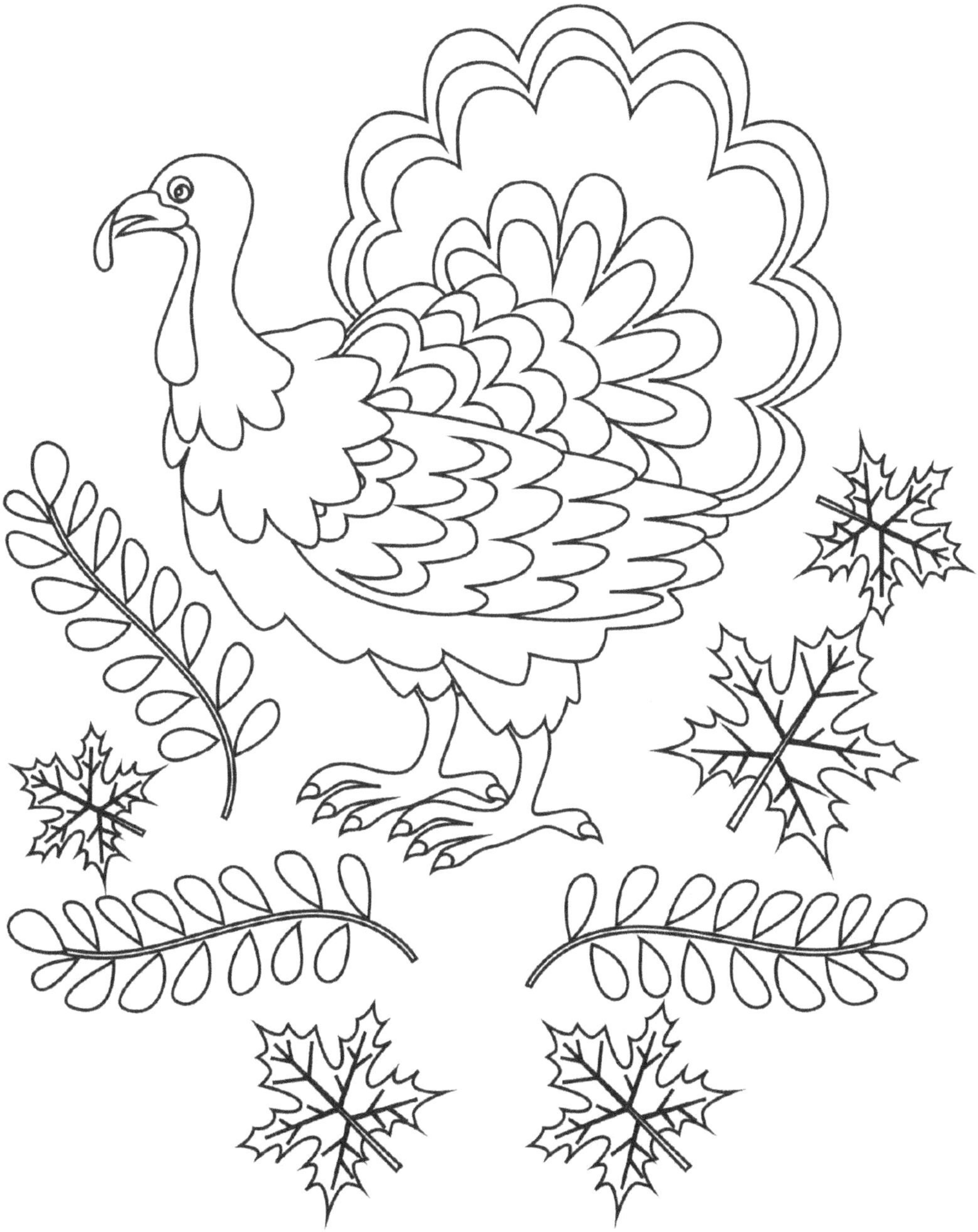

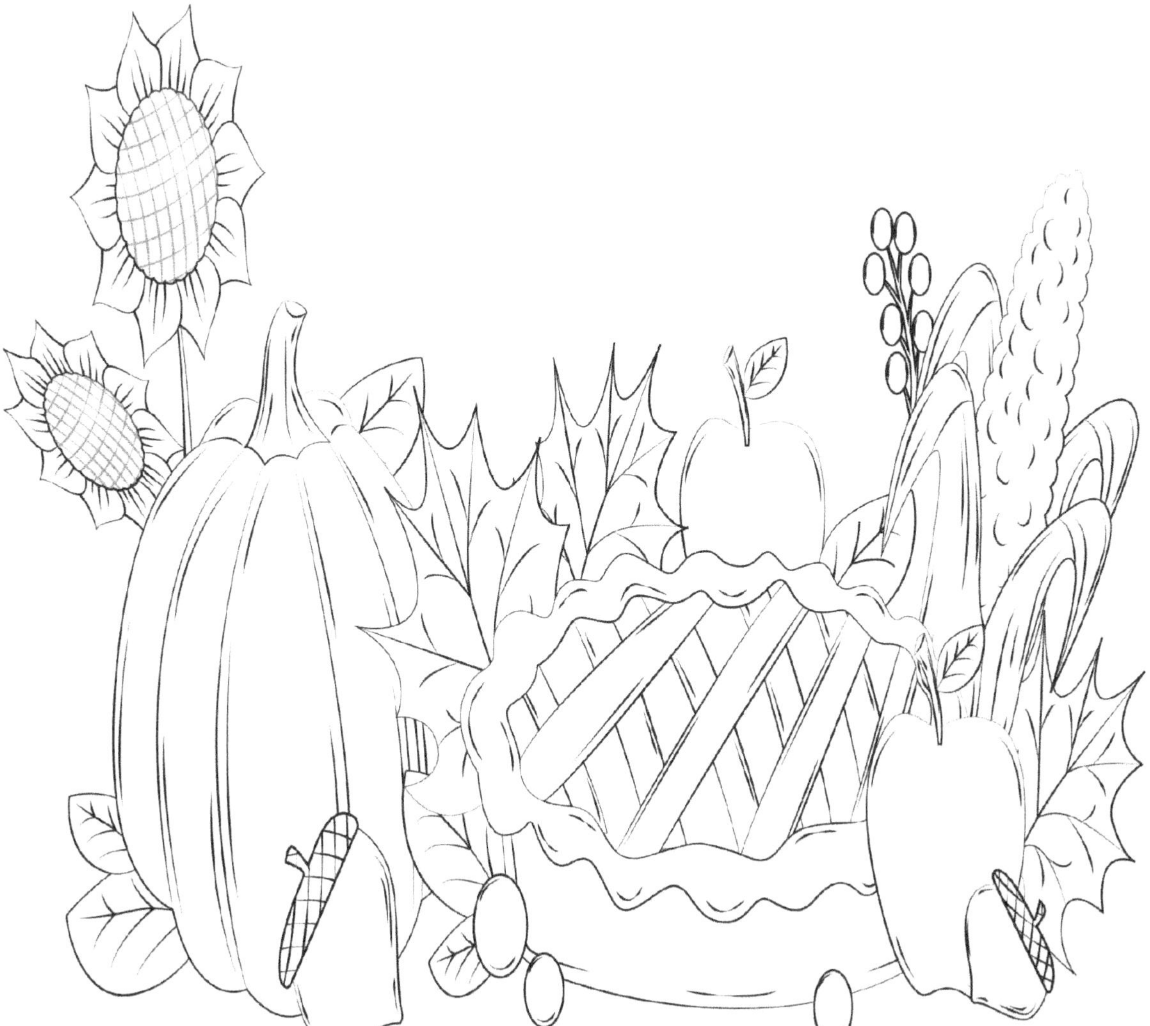

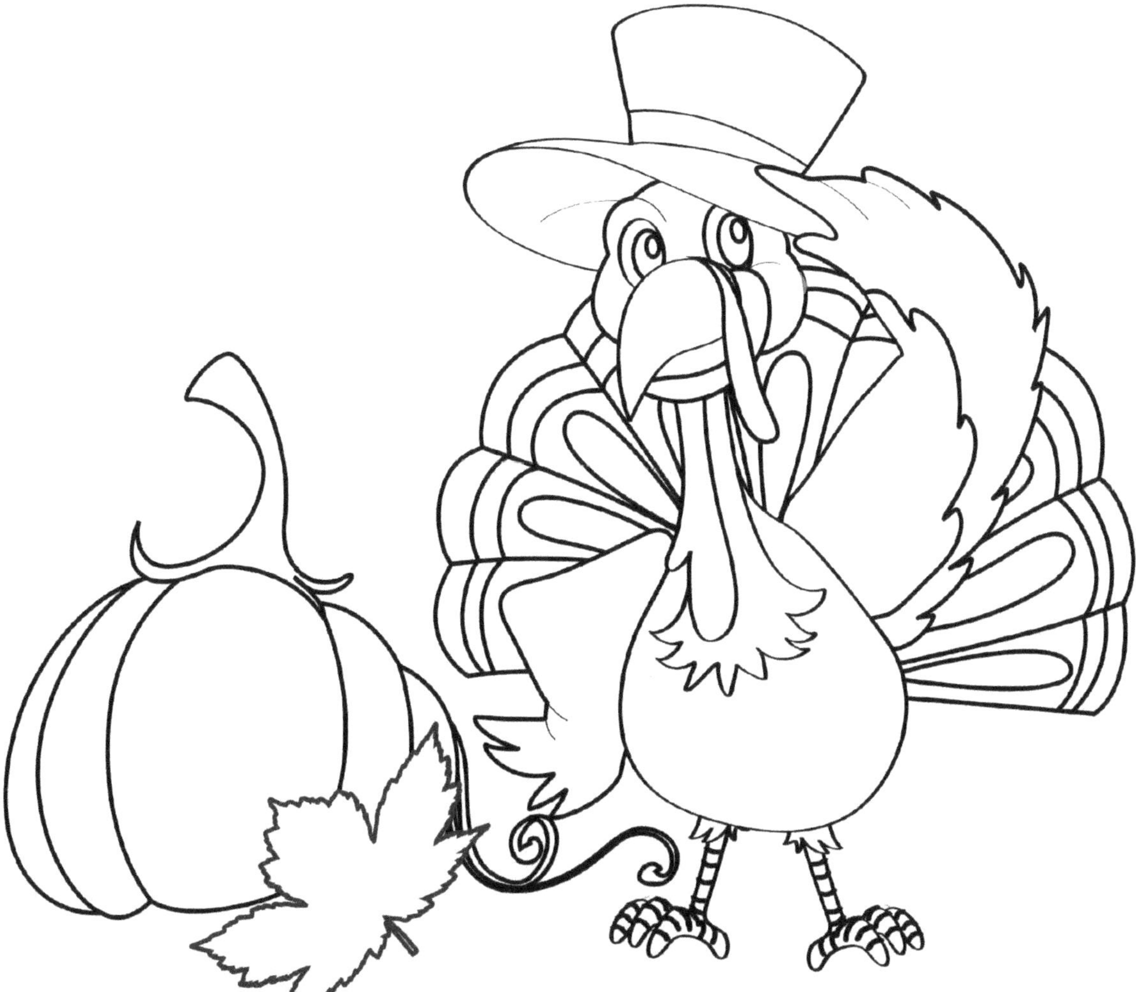

Lightning Source UK Ltd.
Milton Keynes UK
UKHW050913270521
384471UK00008B/511